R3139

Francis Frith's
GLASTONBURY

Photographic Memories

Francis Frith's
GLASTONBURY

Steve Wallis

First published in the United Kingdom in 2001 by
Frith Book Company Ltd

Paperback Edition 2001
ISBN 1-85937-338-0

Hardback Edition 2001
ISBN 1-85937-407-7

British Library Cataloguing in Publication Data

Francis Frith's Glastonbury
Steve Wallis

Frith Book Company Ltd
Frith's Barn, Teffont,
Salisbury, Wiltshire SP3 5QP
Tel: +44 (0) 1722 716 376
Email: info@francisfrith.co.uk
www.francisfrith.co.uk

Printed and bound in Great Britain

Front Cover: High Street, 1896 38373

AS WITH ANY HISTORICAL DATABASE THE FRITH ARCHIVE IS CONSTANTLY BEING CORRECTED AND IMPROVED
AND THE PUBLISHERS WOULD WELCOME INFORMATION ON OMISSIONS OR INACCURACIES

Contents

FRANCIS FRITH, Victorian founder of the world-famous photographic archive, was a devout Quaker and a highly successful Victorian businessman, philosophic by nature and pioneering in outlook.

By 1855 Francis Frith had already established a wholesale grocery business in Liverpool, and sold it for the astonishing sum of £200,000, which is the equivalent today of over £15,000,000. Now a multi-millionaire, he was able to indulge his passion for travel. As a child he had pored over travel books written by early explorers, and his fancy and imagination had been stirred by family holidays to the sublime mountain regions of Wales and Scotland. 'What a land of spirit-stirring and enriching scenes and places!' he had written. He was to return to these scenes of grandeur in later years to 'recapture the thousands of vivid and tender memories', but with a different purpose. Now in his thirties, and captivated by the new science of photography, Frith set out on a series of pioneering journeys to the Nile regions that occupied him from 1856 until 1860.

INTRIGUE AND ADVENTURE

He took with him on his travels a specially-designed wicker carriage that acted as both dark-room and sleeping chamber. These far-flung journeys were packed with intrigue and adventure. In his life story, written when he was sixty-three, Frith tells of being held captive by bandits, and of fighting 'an awful midnight battle to the very point of surrender with a deadly pack of hungry, wild dogs'. Sporting flowing Arab costume, Frith arrived at Akaba by camel seventy years before Lawrence, where he encountered 'desert princes and rival sheikhs, blazing with jewel-hilted swords'.

During these extraordinary adventures he was assiduously exploring the desert regions bordering the Nile and patiently recording the antiquities and peoples with his camera. He was the first photographer to venture beyond the sixth cataract. Africa was still the mysterious 'Dark Continent', and Stanley and Livingstone's historic meeting was a decade into the future. The conditions for picture taking confound belief. He laboured for hours in his wicker darkroom in the sweltering heat of the desert, while the volatile chemicals fizzed dangerously in their trays. Often he was forced to work in remote tombs and caves where conditions were cooler. Back in London he exhibited his photographs and was 'rapturously cheered' by members of the Royal Society. His reputation as a photographer was made overnight. An eminent modern historian has likened their impact on the population of the time to that on our own generation of the first photographs taken on the surface of the moon.

VENTURE OF A LIFE-TIME

Characteristically, Frith quickly spotted the opportunity to create a new business as a specialist publisher of photographs. He lived in an era of immense and sometimes violent change. For the poor in the early part of Victoria's reign work was a drudge and the hours long, and people had precious little free time to enjoy themselves. Most had no transport other than a cart or gig at their disposal, and had not travelled far beyond the boundaries of their own town or village.

However, by the 1870s, the railways had threaded their way across the country, and Bank Holidays and half-day Saturdays had been made obligatory by Act of Parliament. All of a sudden the ordinary working man and his family were able to enjoy days out and see a little more of the world.

With characteristic business acumen, Francis Frith foresaw that these new tourists would enjoy having souvenirs to commemorate their days out. In 1860 he married Mary Ann Rosling and set out with the intention of photographing every city, town and village in Britain. For the next thirty years he travelled the country by train and by pony and trap, producing fine photographs of seaside resorts and beauty spots that were keenly bought by millions of Victorians. These prints were painstakingly pasted into family albums and pored over during the dark nights of winter, rekindling precious memories of summer excursions.

THE RISE OF FRITH & CO

Frith's studio was soon supplying retail shops all over the country. To meet the demand he gathered about him a small team of photographers, and published the work of independent artist-photographers of the calibre of Roger Fenton and Francis Bedford. In order to gain some understanding of the scale of Frith's business one only has to look at the catalogue issued by Frith & Co in 1886: it runs to some 670 pages, listing not only many thousands of views of the British Isles but

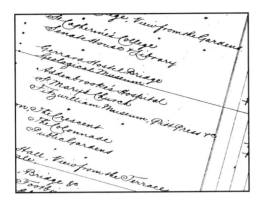

also many photographs of most European countries, and China, Japan, the USA and Canada – note the sample page shown above from the hand-written *Frith & Co* ledgers detailing pictures taken. By 1890 Frith had created the greatest specialist photographic publishing company in the world, with over 2,000 outlets – more than the combined number that Boots and W H Smith have today! The picture on the right shows the *Frith & Co* display board at Ingleton in the Yorkshire Dales. Beautifully constructed with mahogany frame and gilt inserts, it could display up to a dozen local scenes.

POSTCARD BONANZA

The ever-popular holiday postcard we know today took many years to develop. In 1870 the Post Office issued the first plain cards, with a pre-printed stamp on one face. In 1894 they allowed other publishers' cards to be sent through the mail with an attached adhesive halfpenny stamp. Demand grew rapidly, and in 1895 a new size of postcard was permitted called the court card, but there was little room for illustration. In 1899, a year after

Frith's death, a new card measuring 5.5 x 3.5 inches became the standard format, but it was not until 1902 that the divided back came into being, with address and message on one face and a full-size illustration on the other. *Frith & Co* were in the vanguard of postcard development, and Frith's sons Eustace and Cyril continued their father's monumental task, expanding the number of views offered to the public and recording more and more places in Britain, as the coasts and countryside were opened up to mass travel.

Francis Frith died in 1898 at his villa in Cannes, his great project still growing. The archive he created continued in business for another seventy years. By 1970 it contained over a third of a million pictures of 7,000 cities, towns and villages. The massive photographic record Frith has left to us stands as a living monument to a special and very remarkable man.

FRANCIS FRITH's legacy to us today is of immense significance and value, for the magnificent archive of evocative photographs he created provides a unique record of change in 7,000 cities, towns and villages throughout Britain over a century and more. Frith and his fellow studio photographers revisited locations many times down the years to update their views, compiling for us an enthralling and colourful pageant of British life and character.

We tend to think of Frith's sepia views of Britain as nostalgic, for most of us use them to conjure up memories of places in our own lives with which we have family associations. It often makes us forget that to Francis Frith they were records of daily life as it was actually being lived in the cities, towns and villages of his day. The Victorian age was one of great and often bewildering change for ordinary people,

and though the pictures evoke an impression of slower times, life was as busy and hectic as it is today. We are fortunate that Frith was a photographer of the people, dedicated to recording the minutiae of everyday life. For it is this sheer wealth of visual data, the painstaking chronicle of changes in dress, transport, street layouts, buildings, housing, engineering and landscape that captivates us so much today. His remarkable images offer us a powerful link with the past and with the lives of our ancestors.

TODAY'S TECHNOLOGY

Computers have now made it possible for Frith's many thousands of images to be accessed almost instantly. In the Frith archive today, each photograph is carefully 'digitised' then stored on a CD Rom. Frith archivists can locate a single photograph amongst thousands within seconds. Views can be catalogued and sorted under a variety of categories of place and content to the immediate benefit of researchers. Inexpensive reference prints can be created for them at the touch of a mouse button, and a wide range of books and other printed materials assembled and published for a wider, more general readership - in the next twelve months over a hundred Frith local history titles will be published! The day-to-day workings of the archive are very different from how they were in Francis Frith's time: imagine the herculean task of sorting through eleven tons of glass negatives as Frith had to do to locate a particular

See Frith at www.francisfrith.co.uk

sequence of pictures! Yet the archive still prides itself on maintaining the same high standards of excellence laid down by Francis Frith, including the painstaking cataloguing and indexing of every view.

It is curious to reflect on how the internet now allows researchers in America and elsewhere greater instant access to the archive than Frith himself ever enjoyed. Many thousands of individual views can be called up on screen within seconds on one of the Frith internet sites, enabling people living continents away to revisit the streets of their ancestral home town, or view places in Britain where they have enjoyed holidays. Many overseas researchers welcome the chance to view special theme selections, such as transport, sports, costume and ancient monuments.

We are certain that Francis Frith would have heartily approved of these modern developments, for he himself was always working at the very limits of Victorian photographic technology.

THE VALUE OF THE ARCHIVE TODAY

Because of the benefits brought by the computer, Frith's images are increasingly studied by social historians, by researchers into genealogy and ancestory, by architects, town planners, and by teachers and schoolchildren involved in local history projects. In addition, the archive offers every one of us a unique opportunity to examine the places where we and our families have lived and worked down the years. Immensely successful in Frith's own era, the archive is now, a century and more on, entering a new phase of popularity.

THE PAST IN TUNE WITH THE FUTURE

Historians consider the Francis Frith Collection to be of prime national importance. It is the only archive of its kind remaining in private ownership and has been valued at a million pounds. However, this figure is now rapidly increasing as digital technology enables more and more people around the world to enjoy its benefits.

Francis Frith's archive is now housed in an historic timber barn in the beautiful village of Teffont in Wiltshire. Its founder would not recognize the archive office as it is today. In place of the many thousands of dusty boxes containing glass plate negatives and an all-pervading odour of photographic chemicals, there are now ranks of computer screens. He would be amazed to watch his images travelling round the world at unimaginable speeds through network and internet lines.

The archive's future is both bright and exciting. Francis Frith, with his unshakeable belief in making photographs available to the greatest number of people, would undoubtedly approve of what is being done today with his lifetime's work. His photographs, depicting our shared past, are now bringing pleasure and enlightenment to millions around the world a century and more after his death.

Glastonbury lies in eastern Somerset, about 20 miles south of Bristol and a similar distance north-east of Somerset's county town, Taunton. It is in a prominent location in what strikes the visitor as a rather odd landscape with tracts of flat countryside interrupted by steep hills rising abruptly from them.

The flatlands are the Somerset Levels, areas which, until modern drainage methods were used, were marshy and prone to flooding. These conditions led to the formation of layers of peat, which has played an important part in the local economy. In the past, peat was cut by hand and dried out for use as fuel. Today in some areas the peat is stripped by machinery, mainly for use by gardeners, but since the importance of the Levels for wildlife is now recognised, other areas are kept flooded. Also, the waterlogged conditions of the Levels have preserved archaeological remains that do not normally survive elsewhere - materials such as wood and leather. Important archaeological sites include the Iron Age lake villages at Glastonbury and a number of prehistoric trackways.

There are two main ranges of hills in the Glastonbury area, both running eastwards from close to the Bristol Channel. The larger range is that of the Mendips to the north, forming a spectacular backdrop to many views across the Levels. The other is the Polden Hills, cutting across the Levels a little south of Glastonbury.

However, the most spectacular and unusual hill in the area belongs to neither range. This is Glastonbury Tor, which in reality is linked to high ground to the east but which, from some angles, rises like a cone from the Levels. As a landmark, the Tor is enhanced considerably by the tower on its top, belonging to the Medieval church of St Michael. In legend, Glastonbury has been linked with King Arthur's Isle of Avalon - today it can seem odd that it was seen as an Isle, but in the past when the area was even

Shapwick, Turfing in Somerset 1904 52060

Shapwick lies a few miles west of Glastonbury, but this scene could be almost anywhere on the Levels. Turves are being piled on the cart, while the ground from which they have been cut is on the left. There are piles of cut turves behind the horse.

more prone to flooding than today, the Tor must have looked like an island in the Levels.

Glastonbury is still a place of legends. Besides connections with Arthur, there is a story that Joseph of Arimathea, in whose tomb Jesus was buried, came here as a trader and brought the Glastonbury Thorn. It is now thought that this legend was concocted around the 13th century by the monks of Glastonbury Abbey, which forms the subject of the next chapter.

Today the Abbey, the Tor and the mystic associations of Glastonbury attract many visitors, but the photographs of the town in the Francis Frith Collection show it when it was much more of a simple market town.

This volume also looks at some other towns and villages, within a radius of a little under ten miles from Glastonbury, which are also represented in the Francis Frith Collection. Some of these places are in, or on the edge of, the Levels, others are in the hilly areas to the south and east of Glastonbury. Many have historic connections with Glastonbury because of the increasing wealth through the Middle Ages of its Abbey, and the Abbots in particular, who held large swathes of land in the area, and built themselves residences here and there, and barns to collect their share of their tenants' produce.

Shapwick, Wheeling out the Turf 1904 52063

The Abbey Gateway 1909
61545

The Lodge is on the left. The building on the right is the Town Hall, constructed eight years after the restoration of the Gatehouse. Note that it was covered with ivy and had no clock when this photograph was taken. A superb car is in front of the gateway - is the man in white on the left a chauffeur?

It might seem that ruins like the Abbey can only decay, but the photographs of the Francis Frith Collection give a fascinating and valuable insight into the conservation and restoration work on the Abbey that has taken place over the last century or so.

First a little about the history of the place. It has been suggested that the Abbey might date from the time of British Christianity before Somerset was conquered by the Saxons, but otherwise it was founded by King Ine of Wessex in the early 8th century. The most influential individual in the early development of the Abbey was Dunstan, born nearby at Baltonsborough and Abbot from 940 to 956. He extended the buildings and reformed the monks' lifestyle with the introduction of the rule of St Benedict.

In 1184 fire destroyed most of the building,

and almost the whole complex had to be rebuilt. The date of rebuilding is usually given as 1186, although in reality it must have been spread over several years. The Abbey, and its Abbots, grew increasingly wealthy over the centuries, and Glastonbury was one of the main targets of Henry VIII's Dissolution of the Monasteries in the 1530s. Thereafter much of the stonework of the abandoned Abbey was robbed for re-use elsewhere. In 1907 the site was bought on behalf of the Church of England.

Between 1908 and 1979, a series of archaeological excavations on the Abbey site exposed much of the structure that was entirely below ground a century ago. F Bligh Bond and C A Ralegh Radford were two of the main excavation directors. Some of the excavated areas have been left open, while elsewhere the results of excavation and extrapolation have allowed concrete settings to be laid on the lines of walls that have gone completely, making it easier to understand the plan of the whole building. In 1993, a new visitors centre was opened.

Since the photographs of the Francis Frith Collection mainly record the ruins that have remained standing, we shall concentrate on these in this chapter.

The visitor enters through the Abbey's Medieval Gatehouse, which was built in the mid-14th century and restored in 1810. The original arched entrance survives, but an upper storey of the Gatehouse has been lost. Beside it is the Lodge, which had a two-storey bay window added in the 17th century. A date of 1926 on one of the Lodge's rainwater heads presumably records restoration work.

Right: The Abbey from the East 1927 80562

A good view along the length of the Abbey looking from east to west. The footings in the foreground belong to the Edgar Chapel, excavated only a few years before this photograph was taken. The chapel was begun by Abbot Richard Bere and completed by Richard Whiting, the last Abbot. The top of the tower on St Benedict's church can just be made out in the distance.

Right: The Abbey, The Holy Thorn c1955 G12051

The metal sign stating 'Glastonbury Thorn - The Original Thorn Grew on Wyrral Hill' is still there, but the thorn itself now needs two supports. The building behind is now known as St Patrick's Chapel. This chapel and an entranceway are all that remain of the Medieval hospital of St John the Baptist, which cared for the poor and infirm, and which Abbot Bere refounded in 1512 as almshouses.

Right: The Abbey 1890
23910

Photographs 23910, 38376, 64487 and 64486 focus on the transept, which can be described as the arms of the cross-shaped Abbey church. This is a good general view, with the walls of the transept and, between them, in the distance is Abbey House, constructed in the mid-19th century. The south wall of the nave is on the right.

Above: **The Abbey 1896** 38376

A closer view of the transept. A seat has appeared in the intervening six years since 23910 was taken - it and the steps beside it have gone today, the latter replaced by a shallow bank of earth as before, and now gone. Comparison of this view with that seen today shows that some features have been restored inside the arch of the second storey of the left-hand wall.

Right: **The Abbey, Transept arches 1912** 64487

A detail of the wall on the right in the previous photograph. The wooden scaffolding suggests either a danger of collapse or that building work is in progress. Today this section of wall is bigger and with more architectural detail than in this photograph, suggesting that masonry which had previously collapsed was in the process of being rebuilt.

**The Abbey,
Transept arches
1912** 64486

A view looking
from the north
along the line of
the walls shown
previously. The
Chapel of
St Thomas the
Martyr (better
known as Thomas
à Becket) is
through the end-
on archway to the
left. The main
differences today,
apart from the
dress of visitors
such as the couple
in the photograph,
are the presence of
a path and
concrete outlines
of lost bits of wall.

A nice view with an illusion taken within the choir east of the transept. On first glance, it appears the tree is supported by poles - in fact this is scaffolding supporting the length of wall immediately behind it.

The Lady Chapel is also known as St Mary's Chapel, and just to confuse matters further it is popularly known as St Joseph's Chapel - 'Joseph' being Joseph of Arimathea who was said in legend to have visited Glastonbury, rather than Joseph the husband of Mary. In fact, it is thought that St Joseph's Chapel may have been the chapel in the crypt below the Lady Chapel. This crypt was constructed around 1500 when Richard Bere was Abbot. A record of 1724 states that the crypt was constantly full of water, then it was cleared in 1825. This photograph is a good general view of the chapel looking from the north-west. Not much has changed since the photograph was taken, although some of the trees and vegetation has been removed. There is a date of 1909 on some of the stonework of the right-hand corner, a record of the year in which this stone was reconstructed.

The Abbey, St Joseph's Chapel 1904 52051

An internal view taken from the western end. The covering of foliage makes for a very picturesque structure, but the roots of such foliage must have been causing considerable damage to the stonework.

Far Left: The Abbey, 1906 54478

A reverse view from that in 52051, showing work then in progress on the Chapel. Scaffolding is in place on the left and at the rear for repair work to the masonry, and much of the foliage shown in the previous photograph has gone.

Left: The Abbey, St Joseph's Chapel, Doorway 1912 64482

The doorway on the south side with the north doorway visible through it. Even in black and white, the dirtiness of the stonework shows. There are railings across each doorway, and no real path, only a trampling of the general area by those looking over the railings.

Above: The Abbey, St Joseph's Chapel, Altar of Joseph of Arimathea, 1927
80576

Looking at the site of the altar, the place looks rather run-down, with pieces of masonry stone scattered about at the sides. The vault over the altar is propped up and the place used for storage.

Below: The Abbey, Norman Doorway c1960 G12073

A view of the opposite doorway. The stonework is cleaner and the inner stonework of the archway has been reconstructed. There are now better visitor facilities - a path with a drain, and a walkway between the two doorways. At that time, the walkway went straight between the two doorways, today it follows around the inner wall of the west end.

Above: The Abbey, The Lady Chapel c1960
G12056

Taken from a position further back than 80576 (note the arches probably added in the 19th century that have since been removed). The site is greatly improved, with a gravel surface and better props around the altar site. Today an actual altar is set here, surrounded by benches.

Left: The Abbey, Holy Well 1909   61548

Rediscovered when the crypt was cleared in 1825. The well is thought to be pre-Norman, but the arch of Norman style over it was probably originally over a window in the main body of the Lady Chapel, and was then set here when later rebuilding work made it superfluous. Today, the well is only visible from the side, so this photograph gives a better view than the visitor gets.

The Abbey, The Abbot's Kitchen 1890 23917

The Abbot's Kitchen dates from the 14th century. It is not only the best preserved building of the Abbey, but also one of the best preserved Medieval kitchens in Europe. It was well designed for its purpose, with the roof angled to take heat and smoke from cookery up and out through the louvre at the top of the conical roof. This photograph was taken from the south-west. The lady in contemporary costume posing at the south door gives a good indication of scale. The louvre openings have had glass put in them at some point, which has since been removed. The tree in front is still there, although of course now much larger.

**The Abbey,
The Abbot's Kitchen
1912** 64484

The interior in almost
its 'raw' state. A roof
truss is stored there, but
little else. Note the
grille-like door in the
north doorway.

Above: The Abbey, Abbot's Kitchen 1927
80580

Exhibits in display cases have now appeared, and a collection of stone sculptural fragments is piled here and there. There is now a central table, and a wooden door has appeared in the south doorway.

Left: The Abbey, Abbot's Kitchen, interior c1960 G12049

Looking towards the south doorway again, where a new door has appeared and the old one has been set to one side. The table now has a mirror enabling visitors to inspect details of the roof, and a new style of display case is in use.

Below: The Abbey, Abbot's Kitchen, interior c1960 G12047 **with detail left**

A reverse view of G12049, looking towards the north doorway. The display case on the far wall exhibits Medieval floor tiles from the site. Today the visitor finds that the central mirror is still there, but otherwise the place is almost back to its 'raw' state, except for interpretation panels on the walls. The loose stonework is now stored in the Abbey Gatehouse Lodge.

Market Place 1896
38371

The window cleaners are working on the Crown Hotel (now the Glastonbury Backpackers Café and Bar). The building next door is a bank, which in 1904 was called Stuckey's Banking Company, and is now Natwest. Then there is the George, with a policeman in front who is perhaps ready to direct any traffic that shows up.

The town of Glastonbury had humble origins as the settlement which grew up outside the Abbey. Various servants of the Abbey and tradespeople who did business with the monks lived here. Gradually the town grew more important in its own right, acting as a market for the surrounding countryside - especially, of course, after Henry VIII's Dissolution of the Monasteries. In a way, the entire Abbey is still to be found here in the town, for after the Dissolution much of the stone of the Abbey buildings was taken down and re-used in construction work in the town.

We will do a tour around the town, at its centre, the Market Square, which is just to one side of the entrance to the Abbey. The four photographs shown give a good indication of the changes here, although the main structures have remained the same, changing only in use and decoration. They also show evidence of the increasing tourist trade.

The centrepiece of the square is the Market Cross, erected in 1846 by the architect Benjamin Ferrey, who also designed some of the main buildings in the then-new holiday resort at Bournemouth, and spent a lot of his career rebuilding churches. The Cross is in the style of an Eleanor Cross and replaced a Medieval example. The photographs show that there used to be railings around the Cross and stone steps - the former have now gone and the latter have been replaced in concrete. The water trough in all four photographs has also been replaced with a concrete example in a new position.

The Cross 1904
52046

In a change in advertising strategy, the biggest lettering on the Crown Hotel now advertises Bass Ales rather than the name of the place itself.

The Cross 1927 80560

Our first sight of a car here. The Crown Hotel now advertises its services in greater detail - the lettering on the front states that it is 'family and commercial' and offers 'hot and cold luncheons, teas and grills'. To its left there is a tobacconist and confectioner (today a gift shop). Across the road the Market Cross Sweet Store occupies a property that is today a jeweller's. This is the first view in which the road has a tarmac surface.

Left: The Cross c1955 G12029

View from just into North Load Street. The railings have now gone, but the stone steps survive. The property on the right calls itself The Abbey Gate and claims to be a '14th-century restaurant' while offering home-made cakes and pastries. It is actually next to the 14th- century Abbey Gate, which is not believed to have ever served food.

Right: The Pilgrim's Inn 1904 52047

One building in particular deserves to be picked out from those around the Market Square. It has had several names, but it is now the George Hotel and Pilgrim's Inn, and is a rare example of a surviving Medieval inn. As the name suggests, it was built for pilgrims to the Abbey, and it was constructed around 1450 by Abbot John Selwood. The three shields over the doorway are the arms of the Abbey and of King Edward IV.

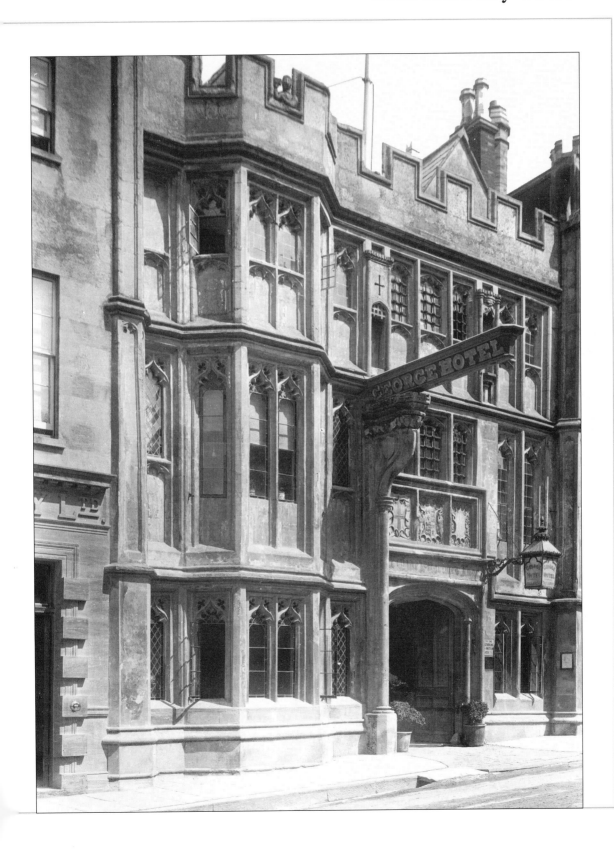

Right: The Bronze Bowl 1890
23906A

An interesting historical document, and an early example of commercial exploitation of archaeology. The bronze object that was being copied by this Taunton company is known as the 'Glastonbury Bowl', and is still considered one of the most important artefacts from the Glastonbury Lake Village.

BRONZE BOWL, ABOUT 2,000 YEARS OLD.

Found on the site of the Prehistoric Lake Village, at Godney, near Glastonbury.

Registered No. 333891.

COPIES IN SILVER AND BRONZE CAN BE OBTAINED OF

FRANKLIN & HARE, PARADE, TAUNTON,

who are, by exclusive permission of the Glastonbury Antiquarian Society,

THE SOLE AUTHORIZED MAKERS.

Left: The Tribunal 1886 19009

Nearby, just into the High Street, there is another building of similar antiquity, the Tribunal. It dates from the early 15th century and is so-called because it was thought to be the courthouse of the Abbots. In fact the earliest use of the name was only in 1791 and the place is now considered to have begun merely as the house of a wealthy local merchant. It was later used by the infamous Judge Jeffreys when he was trying supporters of the Duke of Monmouth after the failure of the Duke's rebellion. The original timber front was replaced with stone around 1500. This is an interesting pre-Museum shot, with the building showing signs of dereliction in the windows and roof. The emblems over the door are the Tudor Rose and the Tudor Royal Arms.

Opposite Above: The Tribunal c1955 G12044

For a time in the 19th century the Tribunal was a school, but it is now a museum, displaying finds from the Glastonbury Lake Village. This site was found by Arthur Bulleid of Glastonbury, who excavated here from 1892 until 1898, then again between 1904 and 1907, this time with Harold St George Gray, curator of the Somerset Archaeological and Natural History Society's museum in Taunton. The site is about a mile north of the town, and is now a series of low mounds. The Lake Village dates from the Iron Age, and was occupied from around 250BC to 50BC, with a maximum population of about 200. One of the two plaques on the wall advertises rates of admission, the other gives historical details of the building.

High Street 1909
61541

Photographs 61541, 38373 and 61542 provide a good series of views taking us down the High Street of about a hundred years ago. Only the last of these show major changes to the buildings in the intervening century, but all show vast differences in the types of businesses. There is a mixture of banks, pubs and shops that is typical of most High Streets of the period, and no indication of the tourist industry. There were obviously far fewer vehicles a hundred years ago, and assuming these photographs were taken on a weekday, fewer people too. The George is on the left, and beyond it what is now Lloyds Bank, built in 1885 but roughly in the same Gothic style as the Medieval inn. The building on the right was then a garage with a passageway through to an open area at the back - today filled with the Glastonbury Experience. Note the roadworks - just a group of men around a hole.

High Street 1896
38373

An earlier view taken a little further up the street. Note the awnings supported on poles shading the shopfronts on this sunny day. The tall building on the left has gone, replaced by that currently occupied by the HSBC bank.

Below: **St. Benedict's Church 1904** 52054

The other church can be called St Benignus' or
St Benedict's. The original dedication was to the obscure
early English St Benignus, also known as Beonna, whose
remains were transferred from Meare to Glastonbury in
1091 by Abbot Turstin. The dedication was later changed,
without the original being forgotten, to St Benedict, the
founder of the Order in the Abbey. Parts of the surviving
structure date from the 14th century, but it was largely
rebuilt by Abbot Bere around 1520, and has his badge on
the porch. The lamppost has since gone. The Mitre Inn,
on the left with a cart in front, has been given a mock
Tudor style in the intervening century.

Above: **High Street 1909** 61542

A view that has changed more
than in the previous two. The
two 18th century buildings on
the left are still there, as is the
smaller one beyond. The next
one, however, has been replaced
by the junction with The
Archers Way. Then, the tall
building belonging to Brooks &
Sons the Drapers, who boast of
being established in 1831, has
been replaced by the Post
Office, which has a datestone
GR 1938.

Right: St. John's Church 1908 61553

Glastonbury has two parish churches, St John's and St Benedict's. They were for the use of the townspeople rather than the Abbey, although the Abbots did carry out work at St Benedict's in particular, and generally their size and wealth of architectural detail are evidence of the wealth of inhabitants of the town rather than of the Abbey. St John's is the most striking feature of the middle High Street and is a major landmark of the town. Saxon burials found in the churchyard suggest an early origin, but the earliest parts that survive date from the 12th century. Features of note include the 15th century Perpendicular tower, 15th-century stained glass reset in two windows of the chancel, and 19th-century furnishings by George Gilbert Scott. This photograph must have been taken from an upper floor of one of the houses across the street. The table-tombs in the churchyard have been rearranged since the photograph was taken. One of the Glastonbury thorns is beside the tower.

Above: St. Benedict's Street 1909 61543
with detail right

Named after the church to which it leads from the Market Square - the church's tower is in the background. The India and China Tea Company's building on the left is now a coffee-house. The Abbey Temperance Hotel next door is a sign of its times. Note the haberdashery on the right advertising Perth Dye Works.

Below: The Tudor Archway, Entrance to St. Mary Magdalene Almshouses 1909 61546

Magdalene Street runs south from the Market Place past the entrance to the Abbey. A little further on the right, and partly hidden away, we find St Mary's Almshouses. Such places were the Medieval version of the Welfare State, and these were founded before 1322 for ten poor men. The present buildings date from a little later in the Middle Ages, but even these are not complete: only the chapel and the end walls, including bell-cote, of the main hall (which formed the living area) survive. After the Middle Ages, the main body of the hall was replaced by two rows of cottages, of which only one range survives. This view is through the archway in the east wall of the former hall beside the chapel entrance. The archway leads to the cottages and garden, but the area through it has been given a roof since this photograph was taken.

The Abbey Barn 1896
38381

Continuing down Magdalene Street and round into Bere Lane, we find the Somerset Rural Life Museum on the corner with Chilkwell Street. It is housed in the Abbey Barn, a 14th century tithe barn in which the monks collected their dues from the surrounding area. It has a cross-shaped plan, and on each of the four gables there is the emblem of one of the four Evangelists - Matthew, Mark, Luke and John. The wall in front, with children perched on it for scale, is still there. Today, in the large panel above the doorway, there are now two stone Medieval windows, presumably brought here from elsewhere.

The east side of the town is overlooked by high ground that includes the Tor and Chalice Hill. One of the more interesting ways to get up here is by the street called Bove Town. Partway up is Jacoby Cottage, which looks like an attractive but otherwise ordinary cottage.

In fact, in the Middle Ages it was the pilgrimage chapel of St James, and although much altered to make it into a habitation, it is the only one of three such outlying chapels in Glastonbury that survives. Higher up, instead of garden walls the properties have enormous slabs of stone acting as buttresses to prevent soil slippage from their gardens into the street.

Above Right: Bove Town 1909 61549

A view up Bove Town, with Jacoby Cottage on the left. The houses here generally date from the 18th and 19th centuries, although the odd one is a century or two older. Some of the houses on the right have now gone.

Right: Bove Town 1908 61550

Looking back down the hill from higher up Bove Town. The nearest house with the unusual diagonal drainpipe arrangement has now gone, making way for Bushy Coombe Gardens, while the middle house of the second terrace is now The Lightship bed and breakfast. Note the slabs of stone.

**From Bushey Coombes
1912 64473**

On the south side of
Bove Town there is a
steep-sided little valley
with the well-deserved
name of Bushy
Coombe. It cuts into
the side of Chalice Hill,
which takes its name
from the famous
Chalice Well on its
other side. This view is
from the side of Chalice
Hill above what is now
Bushy Coombe
Gardens. The area was
and is almost a park,
and we can see the
locals using it in such a
way as a place to sit and
read.

Above: From Chalice Hill 1912 64472

The house in the foreground is Abbey House, and the Abbey and tower of St John's are prominent in the middle distance. Chalice Well is a natural well that was the water source for the early occupants of the Tor. Chalice may be a corruption of Chalkwell, an earlier form of Chilkwell that survives as the name of the street from the town to the area of the well.

Above: The Tor 1896 38382

A view from the north. The Tor is a very distinctive landmark for many miles in most directions. Archaeologists have found evidence of occupation of the hill in prehistory and during the Roman period. There was also occupation in the centuries after the Roman period, but it is not clear if this was a defended civil settlement, perhaps the stronghold of a local chieftain, or a monastic site pre-dating the Abbey. After the Abbey was founded, the Tor continued to be used by religious hermits, then the church of St Michael was built in the 13th century. During Henry VIII's Dissolution, the Tor was the site where the last Abbot, Richard Whiting, and two fellow monks were hung, drawn and quartered.

St. Michael's Tower 1896 38383

The tower dates from the 13th century. In later centuries, the church on the Tor was robbed of its stone, just as the Abbey was. Only the tower, which could not be dismantled so easily, survived. However, although the tower looks complete today, 18th century illustrations show that sections had collapsed, and so restoration work has been needed. The surrounding railing and benches have gone, but this still a great place to sit and admire views of the Somerset countryside.

Left: Wearyall Hill 1896 38384

Now around to the south-west side of Glastonbury, where Wearyall Hill lies between the town and the river Brue. The name is a corruption of 'Wirral Hill', a deer-park established by the Abbots. This view, from the north, is across countryside, whereas today the foreground is occupied by housing and an industrial estate. The Glastonbury Thorn on the hilltop left of the wood is missing from the photograph. Although this is said to be the original Thorn, the photograph shows how it needs to be re-grafted every century or so.

Below: General View 1890 23905

The two church towers belonging St Benedict's (on the left) and St John's are the main landmarks. Note the open countryside flanking the road in the foreground.

Glastonbury, From Wearyall Hill 1904
52042

Taken from the same location on the lower slopes of Wearyall Hill as 23905, this view clearly shows the expansion of the town which has taken place in the intervening fourteen years. Although the angle is slightly different, the hedge in the foreground is the same one. Suburban development has now begun to spread along the road.

n this chapter we look at two market towns of the area, both of which are represented in the collection by some interesting historic photographs.

Street is a town just to the south of Glastonbury across the valley of the river Brue. Street was a common Saxon name for places on Roman roads, and in this case it could be a road running north from the Roman town at Ilchester.

One of Street's claims to fame is that the first skirmish of the Civil War was fought at Marshall's Elm, which is on the ridge of the Poldens above the town. The encounter was won by the Royalists. Today its main such claim is the presence of C & J Clark's shoe factory, a major employer since the 19th century, whose owners have had a major impact on the architecture of the town.

A tour through Street should begin at Holy Trinity parish church, which lies near the northern end of the town not far from the river Brue. The earliest parts of the building date from the 14th century, and there is a squat tower whose height is greatly increased by the weathervane on top. The visitor is struck by the enormous and spacious churchyard, and by noticing that, unlike most parish churches, it does not feel like

Street, The Clock Tower 1896 38388

An intriguing photograph - are the men beside the pile of stones carrying out repairs or new construction? It looks as though they may be finishing work on the wall in the foreground, perhaps linked to the new frontage for the main building constructed around this time. The wall was probably demolished when the factory was extended in 1933.

Street, The Crispin Hall 1896 38389

The Clarks tried to improve the lives of their employees and other residents of the town.
One manifestation of this was the construction of The Crispin Hall which was paid for by William Clark and designed by Skipper. It opened on 12 October 1885. It had a hall, lecture and reading rooms, a library and a museum. The name is appropriate to a place built by the Clark family - St Crispin was the patron saint of shoemakers! Built in the Victorian Gothic style, with chimneys in Tudor style, the front has the simple inscription 'Club and Library 1885'. Today, there are only minor differences to the exterior of the building, but inside it is used by a number of small businesses as well as for community uses.

you are in the historic core of the town. Apart from an old industrial building now converted to housing and a few cottages, it is surrounded by 20th-century development.

Moving down the High Street, we find a town centre greatly influenced by the shoe factory of C & J Clark. Today, Clark's Shopping Village attracts many visitors, but the shoe factory is still there. The business was founded in 1825, and developed through the 19th century, and its success is reflected in the development of its

headquarters. This was built in 1857, then, in 1887, a favourite architect of the Clark family, G T Skipper, constructed the clock tower we see in photograph 38388. It was said to be based on an example at Thun in Switzerland.

In the 1890s, William Reynolds was commissioned to redesign the frontage and to construct a water tower to the rear. This is six storeys high and has on its side the words 'C & J Clark established 1825' above an image of St Michael's tower on Glastonbury Tor.

**Street, General View
1896** 38386

The Clark family also had a major influence on the architecture of the rest of the town. They built housing for their employees in their own style, and many of the shops of the High Street also reflect their style. This view down the High Street from just south of the Crispin Hall shows a number of buildings of this type, particularly those on the right with the tall front gables. Many are still there today, although their frontages have been modernised. Others have been replaced by new buildings copying the Clark style - with varying degrees of success. Most of the shops on the right are still there, but with changes in use. For instance, the one with the projecting sign advertising 'W Herring, ironmonger' is now a shoeshop. The tall building in the background has lost its turret and gained a weathervane. Some of the properties on the left have been replaced by late 20th-century shops.

Somerton lies about five miles directly south of Street, making it the southernmost of the places looked at in this book. For two short periods, it was the county town of Somerset, firstly under the Saxon kings of Wessex in the 7th and 8th centuries, and then from the mid-13th to the mid-14th century.

Somerton was and is a little market town full of old buildings, and any tour of the place must begin at its centre at the Market Cross, or the Buttercross as it is also known. It is recorded that the market was already in existence in 1290, and a century later there is another reference to a Market Cross. The current structure, however, was built in 1673. It has eight sides, with an archway opening through each side and with gargoyles on each corner. Restoration work has taken place on a number of occasions. For instance, a record of 1877 states that the structure had a stone ball and an iron Latin cross on the top. The cross was later lost, and looking at photograph 52500 we see only the ball. Today's visitor sees a replacement cross that was added in recent years.

The Market Square has a number of other attractive buildings, including the 300-year-old Town Hall next to the Market Cross, and behind it other buildings constructed on the site of what had been a castle. One of these, the White Hart Inn, is thought to incorporate masonry from that castle. On the opposite side there is the 'Market House Restaurant', dating from the 16th century. The parish church of St Michael and All Angels is set back from the Square on this side.

Much of the structure of this church, including its octagonal tower, dates from around 1300, but it is best-known for the carved wooden roof, which is a couple of hundred years younger. This roof includes depictions of men and angels, but the dragons are the most spectacular part, and there is even a cider barrel left up there by the builders, either by mistake or as a joke.

Somerton, Market Cross 1904 52500

A scene that is little changed today, except that now there are pipes issuing from the gargoyles and the area around is paved. The house on the left with the delivery cart in front is now plastered. The corner of the Town Hall is on the right.

Above: Somerton, Long Sutton and Langport Roads 1904 52504

Heading back in the opposite direction from the market down West Street, we pass the Unicorn Hotel, which may be Tudor with its distinctive two-storey porch and original doorway. Across the street are the Hext Almshouses, a row of four cottages restored in 1967 carrying the inscription 'EH He Hath Dispersed abroad and Given to the Poor, His Benevolence Remaineth for ever since 1626'. West Street then divides at the point in this photograph which shows why this area is called the Triangle. The shop advertising 'Cycle Goods and Fancy Stores' is now a fish and chip shop, which has extended to the left into the area where is advertised 'Spratt's Patent Dog Cakes' - the nature of which leaves the mind boggling. An auctioneer and valuer is also advertising here.

Below: Somerton, Broad Street 1904 52505 **with detail bottom**

Broad Street runs north from beside the Square. Looking back towards the Market Square we see how it got the name, and it used to be used for a pig market. It has a number of good-quality older buildings, and near the end a silver-painted fountain and horse trough set up in 1902 to commemorate King Edward VII's coronation. The trees are still there, but the quiet scene of two pony and traps and a few children playing is replaced by parked cars on both sides. The building on the right, today an optician's, is the shop of a seedsman, then an important part of the rural economy.

The final chapter takes us on a tour around some of the historic and attractive villages around Glastonbury that are represented in the Francis Frith Collection.

Out on the Somerset Levels to the north-west of Glastonbury, about three miles distant, is Meare, a long village straddling one of the roads which run across the Levels in long straight lengths. In the past it was probably more strung out, with gaps between many of the properties, but modern developments have filled in most of those gaps. Meare belonged to Glastonbury Abbey for most of the latter's existence.

Two more Iron Age lake villages similar to that at Glastonbury have been found here, a little to the north-west of the modern village. The excavations were again carried out by Bulleid and St George Gray, who individually or together, worked here from 1908 to 1956, digging for some of each summer except when the Wars intervened. The villages were in use for roughly the same time period as that at Glastonbury. There is a display of the finds in the County Museum in Taunton.

Several prehistoric trackways have also been found in the area. They were made of laid timbers and allowed people to cross the marshy land of the Levels - signs of a well-organised society. Two, called the Sweet Track and the Post Track, extend from the Shapwick area into Meare parish. Modern dating techniques have shown that the Sweet Track is almost six thousand years old.

The village gets its name from a real 'mere', or lake, called the Meare Pool. It was situated on the south-west bank of this lake, which was some five miles in circumference and which was not drained until the 18th century - after the Reformation when there was no longer a rich Abbot and Abbey living off its produce. The Domesday Book of 1086 records three fisheries and ten fisherman at Meare. In the Middle Ages

Pool, and to identify those in their ownership they painted their own mark on the birds' bills.

The eastern part of the village has a nice grouping of three historic monuments all dating from the Middle Ages - the parish church, Manor Farm and the Abbot's Fish House.

Meare, Abbot's Fish House 1904   52057

The Abbot's Fish House dates from the reign of Edward III early in the 14th century, and is probably linked to other building work at the church and manor, connected with Abbot Adam of Sodbury. Fish were an important part of the monastic diet, particularly as they could be eaten on days when meat was forbidden. Local tradition says it was the house of the chief fisherman or water bailiff, but it is not known if he was a servant of the Abbey or the Abbot himself. The building would also have been used for the salting and storing of fish caught in the adjacent lake. The land here is only just higher than that to the north where the lake was. The irregular ground around the building is a remnant of fishponds that would probably have pre-dated it. The building had a fine open timber roof that was destroyed in a fire in the late 19th century, but some repairs took place in 1893.

Between the Fish House and the parish church there is Manor Farm. This used to be the Manor House for Meare. Before the Reformation it was a summer house of the Abbots of Glastonbury, who built it around 1340 or perhaps a little earlier. The section of the building to the right of the two-storey porch was the main hall in the time of the Abbots. Look closely to see the three original large windows, now blocked with stone.

Below: Meare, Church and Cross c1960 M265014

The parish church in Meare is dedicated to St Mary. The present building was consecrated in 1323 for Adam of Sodbury, and there was later building work by Abbot John Selwood (1456-93) who left his initials on the outer wall of the south aisle. In the churchyard there is a cross, to the left of the avenue of trees, whose only inscription is a date of 1844, high up on the shaft. In fact the shaft belongs to a cross that dates from the 15th century and was originally by the roadside, but which was moved to its present spot at the date of the inscription, when the little cross on the top was also added. Next to the church there is Pelicans F E College, which used to be Ferlingmere House. It may date back to the Middle Ages as a monastic dwelling, and later became the rectory and then the Ring O'Bells Inn. Restoration work to the builing took place in the late 20th century. The door and windows have since been restored to their old style. Opposite the church is Meare School, which has a nice little bell tower with a clock below, and an inscription on the front that explains that the school was built by public subscription (presumably of the villagers) in 1840.

Left: Meare, Abbots Fish House c1960 M265008

Major changes have now taken place since 52057 was taken with much of the work having been carried out around 1920 by The Office of Works. The building has been re-roofed with tiles and protective iron grills have been set in the windows and doorway. A line of paving stones has been laid for visitor access across the often boggy ground.

Above: Meare, The Manor c1960 M265009

A Victorian Gothic building, note the crenellations over the two-storey bay window on the right. The shield over the door says 'Peace On Thy House'. The Manor now offers accommodation and meals.

Right: Meare, Church Path c1960 M265001

Church Path runs parallel with the main road. Here, on the left, we find the non-Conformist church that is now called 'Meare Independent Evangelical Church'; it is built mainly of red brick, with decorative use of buff and black bricks and of stone. The cottages beyond are still there, with the stonework now plastered over. Today the path is covered with tarmac. Further on, there is an area of 19th-century 'suburban' expansion, with several middle-class residences of the time, including an example from around the 1820s that has three storeys with a parapet above and an original porch, and the house called The Manor.

High Ham, Village Green c1965 H508005

This photograph shows the eastern side of the green. The village shop on the right is now a private house and the telephone box outside it has been moved around to the south side, outside The Old Rectory. The Old Rectory was built in the mid-19th century by an architect called John Newton, and is now a school. A bit of the Old School House is just inside the left-hand edge of the photograph.

If we now head about seven miles south from Meare, crossing a stretch of the Levels, then the Polden Hills and then another area of Levels, we find High Ham, about four miles west of Somerton. The village is high indeed, with flat lands of the Levels on all sides except the south-east.

High Ham can boast the last thatched windmill in England, called Stembridge Tower Mill. It is on the south-east side of the village, not surprisingly on Windmill Hill. It was built around 1820, mainly out of the local Lias stone, and its structure incorporated some of the old Ham Mill, which it replaced. The windmill was in use until 1910, and was willed to the National Trust, which now maintains it and opens it to the public at certain times.

The centre of the village is the green, and there are several buildings of interest around it. The house by the north side of the green was once the village school. Free elementary schooling was first offered in the village as early as the late 16th century, when the rector, one Adrian Schael, pulled down the old parish house and built this place as the school. The date of 1598 is given for its construction.

The parish church of St Andrew is set back at the north-west corner of the green. It is thought that Abbot Herlwin of Glastonbury began its construction around the year 1100 (the village belonged to Glastonbury Abbey in the Middle Ages). The tower dates from the reign of Edward III. The nave was rebuilt as a co-operative effort involving Abbot Selwood of Glastonbury and local landowners, including one called Sir Amias Poulett. According to tradition, this work took place all within a single year - 1476. The outside of the nave has an unusual assortment of gargoyles including musicians and a monkey, and a figure over the porch is St Andrew reading a book. The chancel was rebuilt in 1499 by the rector, John Dyer, and at the same time monks from Glastonbury produced the superb rood screen.

Heading north from the green, the visitor passes Manor Farm, which has two projecting wings to the sides which date from the 17th century if not earlier. Then there is an open stretch of road, with a good panorama towards the north and east that includes Glastonbury Tor and Dundon Hill, before the view in photograph H508010 is reached. This is close to the end of the village, where the road begins a steep descent down into the Levels.

If we now follow a line that runs between east and north-east, we pass through three more villages which are represented in the Francis Frith Collection. Firstly, after about four miles, we reach the parish of Compton Dundon. Signs on the main road running south from Glastonbury and Street towards Somerton and Yeovil, inform travellers that they are passing through Compton Dundon; however, the village that the road passes through is simply called Compton, while over the other side of Dundon Hill to the west there is the separate village of Dundon. There is still a strong local feeling that these are two villages which happen to share the same parish.

The parish is on the south side of the Polden Hills, and there are some striking cliffs with exposed bands of red and white stone above the village.

Hidden among the woods on top of Dundon Hill, there is an Iron Age hillfort called Compton Dundon Camp. At its south end there is a mound, some twenty feet high, called Dundon Beacon. This mound was excavated around 1831 by a Mr Hasell. He found what was described as a 'rude cist' - a rough stone setting, enclosing a burial in a kneeling posture together with an urn containing a number of penannular rings. This indicates that the mound is a prehistoric barrow, but

Below: High Ham, Village Green c1965
H508003

Almost a reverse view from H508005, looking towards the west side of the green. It looks as though the car is parked while the driver uses the village shop. There is an old-fashioned Somerset County Council signpost to the car's left. The Old Vicarage, which has Ham stone used around the windows and doorway for an attractive effect, is behind it. The garden wall of the Old School House is in the right foreground.

Right: Dundon, Church and Vicarage 1904
52524

The chancel dates from around 1300, and the renowned writer Sir Nikolaus Pevsner calls it 'remarkable'. Much of the rest, including the tower, is built in the Perpendicular style of the 15th century. Next to the church is the Old Vicarage, built in 1867. This view has only changed in the amount of vegetation. From this spot today, much of the view is obscured, notably by a fantastic specimen of a yew which has spread its canopy across the churchyard. The vicarage on the left is now hidden behind a high hedge. However, there is now no foliage growing up the tower - perhaps it was removed because of damage that it could cause to the structure. Around the time this photograph was taken, the vicar speculated that there were five to six thousand bodies in the churchyard, most in unmarked graves.

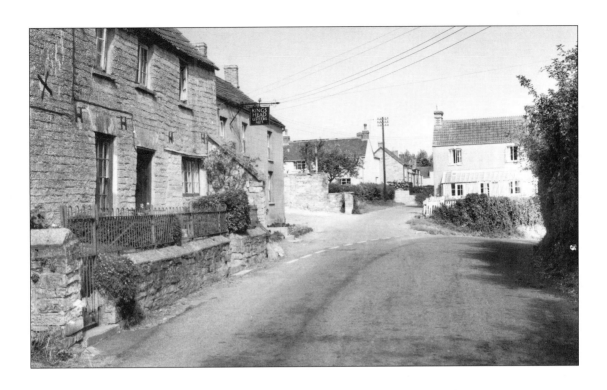

**Above: High Ham,
Village c1965**
H508010

The old cottage at
front left has gone,
being replaced a few
years after this photo-
graph by a bungalow
which is part of St
Andrews Close. The
pub next to it, the
King's Head, is still
there, now advertised
as a Bass Free House
rather than an Ushers
establishment as
then.

there are theories that it may also be a Norman motte (perhaps part of an attempt to remodel the hillfort into a castle), or a beacon or even a supporting mound for a windmill.

Both Compton and Dundon have a number of attractive old stone buildings, and Dundon also has the parish church of St Andrew.

Continuing for another three miles along the straight route that brought us from High Ham to Compton Dundon, we cross back over the Polden Hills and find Butleigh. This village is at the foot of the Poldens and so on the edge of the Levels a few miles south of Glastonbury and south-east of Street.

Our short tour of the place begins at the parish church of St Leonard. It was much restored in the 1850s by an architect called Buckler, although he reused many existing features of the building. There are two features that make the church worth a look around. Firstly, on a window ledge in the south transept there are three kneeling figures taken from an Elizabethan tomb and obviously in contemporary dress. The window itself is surrounded by heraldic devices.

Then, in a side chapel, there is a large monument to the three Hood brothers, sons of the Reverend Samuel Hood of Butleigh. The best known of the three was the eldest, Samuel (1724-1816), who became Viscount Hood. He had a long and distinguished naval career, fighting particularly in the various wars against the French that occurred during his lifetime. In 1795 Horatio Nelson described him as 'the best officer, take him altogether, that England has to boast of'. Another brother, Alexander, also had a distinguished naval career, becoming Viscount Bridport of Cricket St. Thomas. The monument has a long inscription of the type that today we find too tiresome to read, and at the bottom, a depiction of a shipwreck and survivors escaping in a boat.

Above: Butleigh, The Monument c1960
B866006

Back up on the Poldens above the village, this monument is to Samuel Hood. It is on a hilltop among woods, but a sight line looking straight towards Glastonbury Tor was cleared through those woods, enabling each to be seen clearly from the other. Following the long inscription in the church we find that the base of the monument has long and grandiose inscriptions on three sides about Hood and his career. This photograph looks up the sight line towards Glastonbury Tor.

Above: Butleigh The Village c1955 B866001

The Co-operative store on the right has a sign advertising Wall's ice-cream (it is now a house). Note the unusual two-storey bay window, wider at the ground floor of one of the houses.

Above: Butleigh, The Hospital, c1955 B866003

Built for the village in the 19th century, the hospital was set in its own grounds on the south side of the village. According to information on a tapestry in the church, this hospital was 'Endowed by General Sir George Bowles G.C.B. The first stone was laid by Julia Neville Grenville March 6th 1882'. Apart from some more extensions to the right, this building has not changed much. The clock on the porch is still there nearly half a century after this photograph was taken!

Above: Pilton, Village c1955 P383008

A view up St Mary's Lane taken from the churchyard. The first property on the right side of the road, St Mary's cottage, dates from the 16th or 17th century, and has some original windows intact. On the left, the large building is Church House, which has an inscription stating that it was restored in 1892 for parish purposes. The house beyond it has now gone and has been replaced by a bungalow development.

Above: East Pennard, The Rectory c1960 E240001

The Rectory dates from the early 19th century but was built in a Tudor style. This is a view from the garden side of the house. Note the Tudor-style hoodmoulds around the top of the windows, and the little decorative cross on top of the left-hand gable.

Left: Pilton, Village c1960 P383020

Barkle Brothers describe themselves as 'High Class Grocers, Greengrocers and Provisions'. Their building, now occupied by Pilton Stores, began life as an inn in the 18th century, and has a frontage, including the parapet on the top, characteristic of the period. A building of similar age next door is The Crown Inn which is advertising George's Beers, rather than Usher's as it does today. This scene has changed little in the last 40 years despite being on a corner of the main road.

From the churchyard, a house that looks more like a folly can be seen. It has a crenellated tower and enormous Tudor-style chimneys. This is Butleigh Court, built in 1845, which is set within the grounds of a much older house of the same name that once occupied this site.

Butleigh's main street, as shown in photograph B866001 (page 73), has lots of stone cottages, many dating back to the 17th century. One still has a datestone over the door recording 'WK 1699 EC'.

Moving for another five or six miles in the same direction as before, we get to East Pennard, lying in a coombe in the side of Pennard Hill, which is directly east of Glastonbury. Near the highest part of the village is Pennard House, which is Jacobean but which was much altered around 1815, the year of the Battle of Waterloo. There is a little colonnade running along the front of the house. A little lower down we find the church, called 'The Minster Church of All Saints East Pennard'. As usual around here, much of the building dates from the late Middle Ages, and there is a wooden roof inside of the Somerset style. A Medieval wall painting of two angels survives above the chancel arch and the font, dating from around 1170, and has carvings of four strange beasts that may be harpies, and four heads of devils.

Next to the church is the Rectory, now called The Old Rectory, as is usual when the religious incumbent leaves such places.

Below the church and rectory, the village street runs down into the bottom of the coombe, which is full of vegetation and through which runs a little stream that is a tributary of the river Brue. There are a few cottages including one attractive example that is about four hundred years old and which has tiny windows in the front gables.

To reach our final village, Pilton, we must leave our straight route at East Pennard and travel almost due north for a couple of miles or so. Pilton is a large but quite dispersed village beside the Glastonbury to Shepton Mallet road, and we are now some six miles from the former.

The parish church, dedicated to St John the Baptist, developed from the Norman period onward through the Middle Ages, and is down in a dip at the junction of several streets. The church has an attractive Norman south door, with corbels with heads of a bishop and two angels inside the porch. Inside there is an Easter sepulchre, and the nave and north aisle have Somerset-style timber tie-beam roofs with carvings of angels.

Next to the church there is the manor house. It was established in the 13th century as a residence of the Abbots of Glastonbury and added to by them for the next couple of hundred years. After the Dissolution, it passed into private hands and what we see today from the outside is the result of various alterations made during the 17th, 18th and 19th centuries, including some by one of the Earls of Hereford who owned the place in the 17th century. In the yard at the back there is a rare survival, a dovecote dating from the 13th or 14th century.

Pilton, Tithe Barn c1955 P383014

On the southern edge of the village, the Tithe Barn was where Glastonbury Abbey collected its tithes from the land it held at Pilton. It resembles the Abbey Barn in Glastonbury itself and was built at around the same time, in the 14th or 15th century. Like the Abbey Barn, that at Pilton has the symbols of each of the four Evangelists on medallions on each of the four gables. The thatched roof shown in the photograph has been lost, but in 2001 an organisation called The Pilton Barn Trust was working to repair the masonry and provide a new traditional oak-framed roof.

Frith Book Co Titles

www.francisfrith.co.uk

The Frith Book Company publishes over 100 new titles each year. A selection of those currently available are listed below. For latest catalogue please contact Frith Book Co.

Town Books 96 pages, approx 100 photos. County and Themed Books 128 pages, approx 150 photos (unless specified). All titles hardback laminated case and jacket except those indicated pb (paperback).

Amersham, Chesham & Rickmansworth (pb)	1-85937-340-2	£9.99
Ancient Monuments & Stone Circles	1-85937-143-4	£17.99
Aylesbury (pb)	1-85937-227-9	£9.99
Bakewell	1-85937-113-2	£12.99
Barnstaple (pb)	1-85937-300-3	£9.99
Bath (pb)	1-85937419-0	£9.99
Bedford (pb)	1-85937-205-8	£9.99
Berkshire (pb)	1-85937-191-4	£9.99
Berkshire Churches	1-85937-170-1	£17.99
Blackpool (pb)	1-85937-382-8	£9.99
Bognor Regis (pb)	1-85937-431-x	£9.99
Bournemouth	1-85937-067-5	£12.99
Bradford (pb)	1-85937-204-x	£9.99
Brighton & Hove(pb)	1-85937-192-2	£8.99
Bristol (pb)	1-85937-264-3	£9.99
British Life A Century Ago (pb)	1-85937-213-9	£9.99
Buckinghamshire (pb)	1-85937-200-7	£9.99
Camberley (pb)	1-85937-222-8	£9.99
Cambridge (pb)	1-85937-422-0	£9.99
Cambridgeshire (pb)	1-85937-420-4	£9.99
Canals & Waterways (pb)	1-85937-291-0	£9.99
Canterbury Cathedral (pb)	1-85937-179-5	£9.99
Cardiff (pb)	1-85937-093-4	£9.99
Carmarthenshire	1-85937-216-3	£14.99
Chelmsford (pb)	1-85937-310-0	£9.99
Cheltenham (pb)	1-85937-095-0	£9.99
Cheshire (pb)	1-85937-271-6	£9.99
Chester	1-85937-090-x	£12.99
Chesterfield	1-85937-378-x	£9.99
Chichester (pb)	1-85937-228-7	£9.99
Colchester (pb)	1-85937-188-4	£8.99
Cornish Coast	1-85937-163-9	£14.99
Cornwall (pb)	1-85937-229-5	£9.99
Cornwall Living Memories	1-85937-248-1	£14.99
Cotswolds (pb)	1-85937-230-9	£9.99
Cotswolds Living Memories	1-85937-255-4	£14.99
County Durham	1-85937-123-x	£14.99
Croydon Living Memories	1-85937-162-0	£9.99
Cumbria	1-85937-101-9	£14.99
Dartmoor	1-85937-145-0	£14.99
Derby (pb)	1-85937-367-4	£9.99
Derbyshire (pb)	1-85937-196-5	£9.99
Devon (pb)	1-85937-297-x	£9.99
Dorset (pb)	1-85937-269-4	£9.99
Dorset Churches	1-85937-172-8	£17.99
Dorset Coast (pb)	1-85937-299-6	£9.99
Dorset Living Memories	1-85937-210-4	£14.99
Down the Severn	1-85937-118-3	£14.99
Down the Thames (pb)	1-85937-278-3	£9.99
Down the Trent	1-85937-311-9	£14.99
Dublin (pb)	1-85937-231-7	£9.99
East Anglia (pb)	1-85937-265-1	£9.99
East London	1-85937-080-2	£14.99
East Sussex	1-85937-130-2	£14.99
Eastbourne	1-85937-061-6	£12.99
Edinburgh (pb)	1-85937-193-0	£8.99
England in the 1880s	1-85937-331-3	£17.99
English Castles (pb)	1-85937-434-4	£9.99
English Country Houses	1-85937-161-2	£17.99
Essex (pb)	1-85937-270-8	£9.99
Exeter	1-85937-126-4	£12.99
Exmoor	1-85937-132-9	£14.99
Falmouth	1-85937-066-7	£12.99
Folkestone (pb)	1-85937-124-8	£9.99
Glasgow (pb)	1-85937-190-6	£9.99
Gloucestershire	1-85937-102-7	£14.99
Great Yarmouth (pb)	1-85937-426-3	£9.99
Greater Manchester (pb)	1-85937-266-x	£9.99
Guildford (pb)	1-85937-410-7	£9.99
Hampshire (pb)	1-85937-279-1	£9.99
Hampshire Churches (pb)	1-85937-207-4	£9.99
Harrogate	1-85937-423-9	£9.99
Hastings & Bexhill (pb)	1-85937-131-0	£9.99
Heart of Lancashire (pb)	1-85937-197-3	£9.99
Helston (pb)	1-85937-214-7	£9.99
Hereford (pb)	1-85937-175-2	£9.99
Herefordshire	1-85937-174-4	£14.99
Hertfordshire (pb)	1-85937-247-3	£9.99
Horsham (pb)	1-85937-432-8	£9.99
Humberside	1-85937-215-5	£14.99
Hythe, Romney Marsh & Ashford	1-85937-256-2	£9.99

Available from your local bookshop or from the publisher

Frith Book Co Titles (continued)

Ipswich (pb)	1-85937-424-7	£9.99	St Ives (pb)	1-85937415-8	£9.99
Ireland (pb)	1-85937-181-7	£9.99	Scotland (pb)	1-85937-182-5	£9.99
Isle of Man (pb)	1-85937-268-6	£9.99	Scottish Castles (pb)	1-85937-323-2	£9.99
Isles of Scilly	1-85937-136-1	£14.99	Sevenoaks & Tunbridge	1-85937-057-8	£12.99
Isle of Wight (pb)	1-85937-429-8	£9.99	Sheffield, South Yorks (pb)	1-85937-267-8	£9.99
Isle of Wight Living Memories	1-85937-304-6	£14.99	Shrewsbury (pb)	1-85937-325-9	£9.99
Kent (pb)	1-85937-189-2	£9.99	Shropshire (pb)	1-85937-326-7	£9.99
Kent Living Memories	1-85937-125-6	£14.99	Somerset	1-85937-153-1	£14.99
Lake District (pb)	1-85937-275-9	£9.99	South Devon Coast	1-85937-107-8	£14.99
Lancaster, Morecambe & Heysham (pb)	1-85937-233-3	£9.99	South Devon Living Memories	1-85937-168-x	£14.99
Leeds (pb)	1-85937-202-3	£9.99	South Hams	1-85937-220-1	£14.99
Leicester	1-85937-073-x	£12.99	Southampton (pb)	1-85937-427-1	£9.99
Leicestershire (pb)	1-85937-185-x	£9.99	Southport (pb)	1-85937-425-5	£9.99
Lincolnshire (pb)	1-85937-433-6	£9.99	Staffordshire	1-85937-047-0	£12.99
Liverpool & Merseyside (pb)	1-85937-234-1	£9.99	Stratford upon Avon	1-85937-098-5	£12.99
London (pb)	1-85937-183-3	£9.99	Suffolk (pb)	1-85937-221-x	£9.99
Ludlow (pb)	1-85937-176-0	£9.99	Suffolk Coast	1-85937-259-7	£14.99
Luton (pb)	1-85937-235-x	£9.99	Surrey (pb)	1-85937-240-6	£9.99
Maidstone	1-85937-056-x	£14.99	Sussex (pb)	1-85937-184-1	£9.99
Manchester (pb)	1-85937-198-1	£9.99	Swansea (pb)	1-85937-167-1	£9.99
Middlesex	1-85937-158-2	£14.99	Tees Valley & Cleveland	1-85937-211-2	£14.99
New Forest	1-85937-128-0	£14.99	Thanet (pb)	1-85937-116-7	£9.99
Newark (pb)	1-85937-366-6	£9.99	Tiverton (pb)	1-85937-178-7	£9.99
Newport, Wales (pb)	1-85937-258-9	£9.99	Torbay	1-85937-063-2	£12.99
Newquay (pb)	1-85937-421-2	£9.99	Truro	1-85937-147-7	£12.99
Norfolk (pb)	1-85937-195-7	£9.99	Victorian and Edwardian Cornwall	1-85937-252-x	£14.99
Norfolk Living Memories	1-85937-217-1	£14.99	Victorian & Edwardian Devon	1-85937-253-8	£14.99
Northamptonshire	1-85937-150-7	£14.99	Victorian & Edwardian Kent	1-85937-149-3	£14.99
Northumberland Tyne & Wear (pb)	1-85937-281-3	£9.99	Vic & Ed Maritime Album	1-85937-144-2	£17.99
North Devon Coast	1-85937-146-9	£14.99	Victorian and Edwardian Sussex	1-85937-157-4	£14.99
North Devon Living Memories	1-85937-261-9	£14.99	Victorian & Edwardian Yorkshire	1-85937-154-x	£14.99
North London	1-85937-206-6	£14.99	Victorian Seaside	1-85937-159-0	£17.99
North Wales (pb)	1-85937-298-8	£9.99	Villages of Devon (pb)	1-85937-293-7	£9.99
North Yorkshire (pb)	1-85937-236-8	£9.99	Villages of Kent (pb)	1-85937-294-5	£9.99
Norwich (pb)	1-85937-194-9	£8.99	Villages of Sussex (pb)	1-85937-295-3	£9.99
Nottingham (pb)	1-85937-324-0	£9.99	Warwickshire (pb)	1-85937-203-1	£9.99
Nottinghamshire (pb)	1-85937-187-6	£9.99	Welsh Castles (pb)	1-85937-322-4	£9.99
Oxford (pb)	1-85937-411-5	£9.99	West Midlands (pb)	1-85937-289-9	£9.99
Oxfordshire (pb)	1-85937-430-1	£9.99	West Sussex	1-85937-148-5	£14.99
Peak District (pb)	1-85937-280-5	£9.99	West Yorkshire (pb)	1-85937-201-5	£9.99
Penzance	1-85937-069-1	£12.99	Weymouth (pb)	1-85937-209-0	£9.99
Peterborough (pb)	1-85937-219-8	£9.99	Wiltshire (pb)	1-85937-277-5	£9.99
Piers	1-85937-237-6	£17.99	Wiltshire Churches (pb)	1-85937-171-x	£9.99
Plymouth	1-85937-119-1	£12.99	Wiltshire Living Memories	1-85937-245-7	£14.99
Poole & Sandbanks (pb)	1-85937-251-1	£9.99	Winchester (pb)	1-85937-428-x	£9.99
Preston (pb)	1-85937-212-0	£9.99	Windmills & Watermills	1-85937-242-2	£17.99
Reading (pb)	1-85937-238-4	£9.99	Worcester (pb)	1-85937-165-5	£9.99
Romford (pb)	1-85937-319-4	£9.99	Worcestershire	1-85937-152-3	£14.99
Salisbury (pb)	1-85937-239-2	£9.99	York (pb)	1-85937-199-x	£9.99
Scarborough (pb)	1-85937-379-8	£9.99	Yorkshire (pb)	1-85937-186-8	£9.99
St Albans (pb)	1-85937-341-0	£9.99	Yorkshire Living Memories	1-85937-166-3	£14.99

See Frith books on the internet www.francisfrith.co.uk

FRITH PRODUCTS & SERVICES

Francis Frith would doubtless be pleased to know that the pioneering publishing venture he started in 1860 still continues today. A hundred and forty years later, The Francis Frith Collection continues in the same innovative tradition and is now one of the foremost publishers of vintage photographs in the world. Some of the current activities include:

Interior Decoration

Today Frith's photographs can be seen framed and as giant wall murals in thousands of pubs, restaurants, hotels, banks, retail stores and other public buildings throughout the country. In every case they enhance the unique local atmosphere of the places they depict and provide reminders of gentler days in an increasingly busy and frenetic world.

Product Promotions

Frith products are used by many major companies to promote the sales of their own products or to reinforce their own history and heritage. Frith promotions have been used by Hovis bread, Courage beers, Scots Porage Oats, Colman's mustard, Cadbury's foods, Mellow Birds coffee, Dunhill pipe tobacco, Guinness, and Bulmer's Cider.

Genealogy and Family History

As the interest in family history and roots grows world-wide, more and more people are turning to Frith's photographs of Great Britain for images of the towns, villages and streets where their ancestors lived; and, of course, photographs of the churches and chapels where their ancestors were christened, married and buried are an essential part of every genealogy tree and family album.

Frith Products

All Frith photographs are available Framed or just as Mounted Prints and Posters (size 23 x 16 inches). These may be ordered from the address below. From time to time other products - Address Books, Calendars, Table Mats, etc - are available.

The Internet

Already twenty thousand Frith photographs can be viewed and purchased on the internet through the Frith websites and a myriad of partner sites.

For more detailed information on Frith companies and products, look at these sites:

www.francisfrith.co.uk
www.francisfrith.com
(for North American visitors)

See the complete list of Frith Books at:

www.francisfrith.co.uk

This web site is regularly updated with the latest list of publications from the Frith Book Company. If you wish to buy books relating to another part of the country that your local bookshop does not stock, you may purchase on-line.

For further information, trade, or author enquiries please contact us at the address below:
The Francis Frith Collection, Frith's Barn, Teffont, Salisbury, Wiltshire, England SP3 5QP.
Tel: +44 (0)1722 716 376 Fax: +44 (0)1722 716 881   Email: sales@francisfrith.co.uk

See Frith books on the internet www.francisfrith.co.uk

TO RECEIVE YOUR FREE MOUNTED PRINT

Mounted Print
Overall size 14 x 11 inches

Cut out this Voucher and return it with your remittance for £1.95 to cover postage and handling, to UK addresses. For overseas addresses please include £4.00 post and handling. Choose any photograph included in this book. Your SEPIA print will be A4 in size, and mounted in a cream mount with burgundy rule line, overall size 14 x 11 inches.

Order additional Mounted Prints at HALF PRICE (only £7.49 each*)

If there are further pictures you would like to order, possibly as gifts for friends and family, purchase them at half price (no additional postage and handling required).

Have your Mounted Prints framed*

For an additional £14.95 per print you can have your chosen Mounted Print framed in an elegant polished wood and gilt moulding, overall size 16 x 13 inches (no additional postage and handling required).

> *** IMPORTANT!**
> These special prices are only available if ordered using the original voucher on this page (no copies permitted) and at the same time as your free Mounted Print, for delivery to the same address

Frith Collectors' Guild

From time to time we publish a magazine of news and stories about Frith photographs and further special offers of Frith products. If you would like 12 months FREE membership, please return this form.

Send completed forms to:
The Francis Frith Collection, Frith's Barn, Teffont, Salisbury, Wiltshire SP3 5QP

Voucher for FREE and Reduced Price Frith Prints

Picture no.	Page number	Qty	Mounted @ £7.49	Framed + £14.95	Total Cost
		1	Free of charge*	£	£
			£7.49	£	£
			£7.49	£	£
			£7.49	£	£
			£7.49	£	£
			£7.49	£	£

Please allow 28 days for delivery	*** Post & handling**	**£1.95**
Book Title	**Total Order Cost**	**£**

Please do not photocopy this voucher. Only the original is valid, so please cut it out and return it to us.

I enclose a cheque / postal order for £ . . . .
made payable to 'The Francis Frith Collection'
OR please debit my Mastercard / Visa / Switch / Amex card
(credit cards please on all overseas orders)

Number . . . .

Issue No(Switch only) . . . . .Valid from (Amex/Switch) . . . .

Expires . . . . Signature . . . .

Name Mr/Mrs/Ms . . . .

Address . . . .

. . . .

. . . . Postcode . . . .

Daytime Tel No . . . . Valid to 31/12/02

The Francis Frith Collectors' Guild
Please enrol me as a member for 12 months free of charge.

Name Mr/Mrs/Ms . . . .

Address . . . .

. . . .

. . . . Postcode . . . .

Would you like to find out more about Francis Frith?

We have recently recruited some entertaining speakers who are happy to visit local groups, clubs and societies to give an illustrated talk documenting Frith's travels and photographs. If you are a member of such a group and are interested in hosting a presentation, we would love to hear from you.

Our speakers bring with them a small selection of our local town and county books, together with sample prints. They are happy to take orders. A small proportion of the order value is donated to the group who have hosted the presentation. The talks are therefore an excellent way of fundraising for small groups and societies.

Can you help us with information about any of the Frith photographs in this book?

We are gradually compiling an historical record for each of the photographs in the Frith archive. It is always fascinating to find out the names of the people shown in the pictures, as well as insights into the shops, buildings and other features depicted.

If you recognize anyone in the photographs in this book, or if you have information not already included in the author's caption, do let us know. We would love to hear from you, and will try to publish it in future books or articles.

Our production team

Frith books are produced by a small dedicated team at offices in the converted Grade II listed 18th-century barn at Teffont near Salisbury, illustrated above. Most have worked with the Frith Collection for many years. All have in common one quality: they have a passion for the Frith Collection. The team is constantly expanding, but currently includes:

Jason Buck, John Buck, Douglas Burns, Heather Crisp, Isobel Hall, Rob Hames, Hazel Heaton, Peter Horne, James Kinnear, Tina Leary, Hannah Marsh, Eliza Sackett, Terence Sackett, Sandra Sanger, Shelley Tolcher, Susanna Walker, Clive Wathen and Jenny Wathen.